P9-DIJ-202

Consultant, Istar Schwager, holds a Ph.D. in educational psychology
and a master's degree in early childhood education.
She has been an advisor, consultant, and content designer for numerous parenting,
child development, and early learning programs including the *Sesame Street*
television show and magazines.
She has been a consultant for several Fortune 500 companies
and has regularly published articles for parents
on a range of topics.

Louis Weber, C.E.O.
Publications International, Ltd.
7373 North Cicero Avenue
Lincolnwood, Illinois 60646

Manufactured in the U.S.A.

8 7 6 5 4 3 2 1

ISBN 1-56173-483-7

active minds

numbers

PHOTOGRAPHY
George Siede and Donna Preis

CONSULTANT
Istar Schwager, Ph.D.

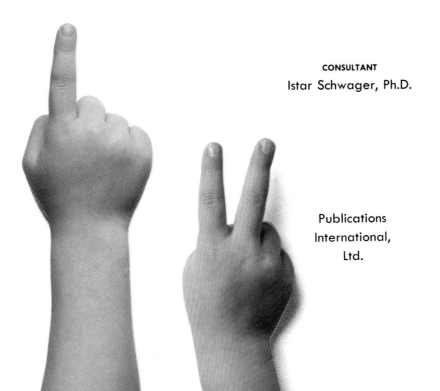

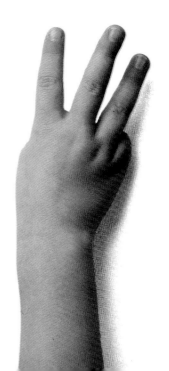

Publications
International,
Ltd.

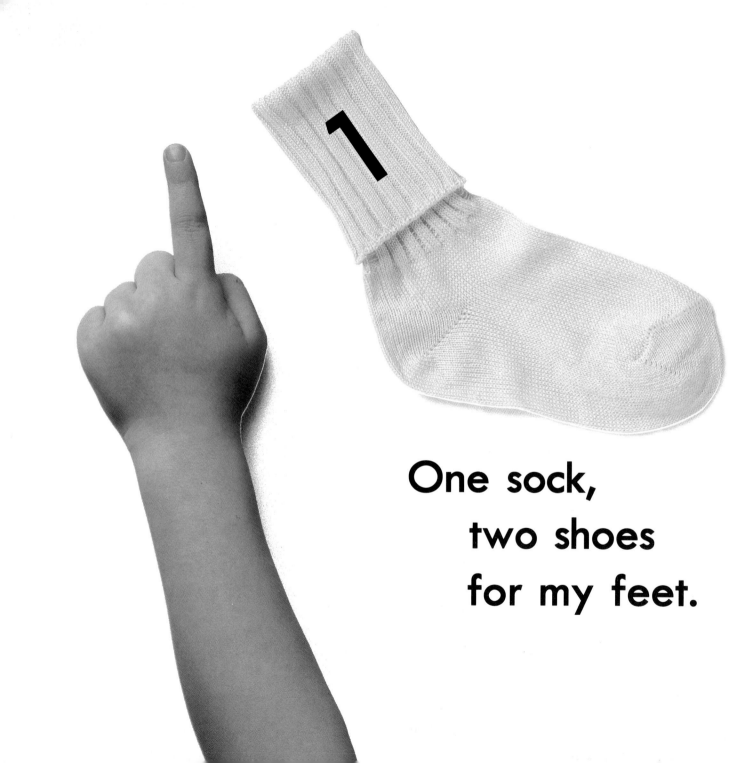

One sock,
two shoes
for my feet.

Three, then

four

1 2

3 4

good things to eat.

Five balloons

up in the sky.

4

5

6

Six ducklings walking by.

Seven flowers standing tall.

1 2 3 4

Eight puppies with a ball.

Nine melons,
juicy and red.

Ten animals
for my bed.

4

5

9

10